This journal belongs to:

_____

Motherhood is the biggest gamble in the world.
It is the glorious life force.
It's huge and scary — it's an act of infinite optimism.

GILDA RADNER

_____
_____
_____
_____
_____
_____
_____
_____
_____
_____
_____
_____
_____
_____
_____
_____
_____
_____
_____
_____
_____
_____
_____

The art of mothering is to teach
the art of living to children.

ELAINE HEFFNER

_Motherhood is a kind of
wilderness through which each woman hacks
her way, part martyr, part pioneer..._

RACHEL CUSK

Sometimes the strength
of motherhood is greater than
natural laws.

BARBARA KINGSOLVER

LIFE
DOESN'T COME
WITH A MANUAL
IT COMES WITH
A MOTHER.

The life of a mother is the life of a chil

you are two blossoms on a single branch.

KAREN MAEZEN MILLER

_____
_____
_____
_____
_____
_____
_____
_____
_____
_____
_____
_____
_____
_____
_____
_____
_____
_____
_____

There's no way to be a perfect mother,

and a million ways to be a good one.

JILL CHURCHILL

Mother is a verb, not a noun.

A mother's love liberates.

MAYA ANGELOU

No language can express the power and beauty and heroism of a mother's love.

EDWIN HUBBELL CHAPIN

However motherhood comes to you, it is a miracle.

SHERYL CROW

The moment a child is born the mother is also born. She never existed before; the woman existed, but the mother, never. A mother is something absolutely new.

RAJNEESH

_____

_____

_____

_____

_____

_____

_____

_____

_____

_____

_____

_____

_____

_____

_____

_____

_____

_____

_____

_____

_____

Mother love is the fuel that enables a normal human being to do the impossible.

MARION C. GARRETTY

The hand that rocks the cradle is the hand that rules the world.

WILLIAM ROSS WALLACE

_____
_____
_____
_____
_____
_____
_____
_____
_____
_____
_____
_____
_____
_____
_____
_____
_____
_____

One thing I had learned from watching chimpanzees with their infants is that having a child should be fun.

JANE GOODALL

_____

_____

_____

_____

_____

_____

_____

_____

_____

_____

_____

_____

_____

_____

_____

_____

_____

_____

_____

Being a mother is learning about strengths you didn't know you had, and dealing with fears you didn't know existed.

LINDA WOOTEN

Mother —that was the bank where we deposited all our hurts and worries.

THOMAS DE WITT TALMAGE

BEING A MOTHER IS AN ATTITUDE NOT A BIOLOGICAL RELATION

ROBERT A. HEINLEIN

There really are places in your heart
you don't even know
existed until you love a child.

ANNE LAMOTT

_____

_____

_____

_____

_____

_____

_____

_____

_____

_____

_____

_____

_____

_____

_____

_____

_____

_____

_____

_____

*There are so many times you will feel
you have failed, but in the eyes, heart and mind
of your child, you are supermom.*

STEPHANIE PRECOURT

An ounce of Mother
is worth a pound of clergy.

RUDYARD KIPLING

Moms
are like buttons: They
hold everything
together

Mother's love is peace.
It need not be acquired, it need not be deserved.

ERICH FROMM

_____

_____

_____

_____

_____

_____

_____

_____

_____

_____

_____

_____

_____

_____

_____

_____

_____

_____

_____

Motherhood is the most challenging as well as the utmost satisfying vocation in this world.

NITA AMBANI

sweater, n. :

GARMENT WORN BY A CHILD
WHEN ITS MOTHER IS FEELING
CHILLY.

AMBROSE BIERCE

If evolution really works, how come mothers only have two hands?

MILTON BERLE

The human heart was not designed to beat outside the human body, and yet, each child represented just that — a parent's heart bared, beating forever outside its chest.

DEBRA GINSBERG